ALEKSANDAR
DURAVCEVIC

STEPPENWOLF

TOTAH

"I am not sure that I exist, actually.
I am all the writers that I have read,
all the people that I have met,
all the women that I have loved;
all the cities I have visited."

— Jorge Luis Borges

Foreword

Aleksandar Duravcevic, known as Sasha, and I met in January of 2015; today our friendship symbolizes the spirit of an enterprise started a little more than a year ago. Our first encounter was marked by my instantaneous obstinacy in acquiring a diptych, two small oils on canvas depicting a full moon in a Tuscan landscape. He was taken aback by my impulsivity but said he couldn't part from it, being the first he had done in that series and medium. I told him that if I woke up the following morning thinking about it, he would have no choice but to allow me to live with it. A few days later the moons became part of the patchwork of imageries that make me feel at "home" in my New York apartment. That episode marked the beginning of a fertile alchemy, which gave birth to 'Steppenwolf'.

When we first discussed his show I broached the idea of making it about the quest for one's identity and for him to interpret the ineffability of that riddle as he wished. From the very beginning I felt a sense of kinship with Sasha and I identified significantly with what, at that time, I felt had been his passage through the vicissitudes of life. We share similar nomadic origins and have crossed dusky steppes where we are meant to remember and recognize the light that we are made of. So far the exhibitions at TOTAH have been a way of expression, created to pass on messages which I am hoping can touch many. I believe that art often can help us understand the complexity of existence by being a metaphor for life, a subtle echo voicing our soul's need to appease its torments and express its joy.

In 'Steppenwolf', Duravcevic walks us through fundamental existential themes in his own poetic and mysterious language, employing his infinitely diverse and rigorous craftsmanship. There is a recurring contrast between the real and the imaginary, time and timelessness, the concrete and the abstract, light and darkness. None of his drawings, sculptures, paintings or altered metal pieces comes to a full stop at the image; they are portals towards another reality, leaving us hungry for more, and forcing us to find our own answers. Like treasures of timeless significance they become antidotes for the mainstream triviality that surrounds us. Many of the images he creates are symbols that transcend the limits of a binary interpretation. He belongs to the category of those artists who offer us clues about the secrets of existence, which everyday life prevents us from seeing. His art represents an interweaving of several worlds made of time and imaginary dwellings; it creates a feeling of being both at home and constantly out of place. The mystique of his work can be preserved only when we surrender to an immediate reaction instead of trying to understand and explain the pathways of his pencil, brush, scalpel or mind.

Although the title of the show was inspired by Herman Hesse's autobiographical allegoric novel, which epitomizes with utter genius the human condition, the actual show is composed of fragments of Duravcevic's own journey; yet one that is universally relevant for those who are seeking. Time, individuality, duality and integration are the main ingredients in our quest for the absolute, the yearning for our own true essence, to finally find our home within ourselves and become whole. It's not a voyage that ends one given day; the arrival may not be where nor what we expect but if there were to be a prize, I'd name it love. A chronic melancholia fuels each step forward, wistfully looking at future odysseys, drawn towards an unknown yet familiar land where unanswered questions find their harbor.

David Totah

Drawing, Repetition, Time

By BARRY SCHWABSKY

It could almost be nothing more than a play on words—to say that, in his drawings, Aleksandar Duravcevic works on a plane of darkness to excavate an unexpected light. What could be more facile than to equate literal and metaphorical darkness and light? Luckily, nothing's quite that simple in Duravcevic's work—a weave of echoes and reflections whose meaning resides less in objects or images than in the resonant space between them. Still, it's clear that this art is rooted in a clear view of the darkness at the heart of our existence—in recognition of the harshness and tragedy of historical experience. This is a universal condition but possibly more vividly present to the imagination of someone who experienced the political crisis and breakup of Yugoslavia and the resulting civil wars than to those of us who have so far been fortunate enough to merely watch such events from a distance. And yet in talking about light and darkness, I am describing a simple question of technique. Duravcevic is an artist of many media—painting, sculpture, video, installation—but as is true of many other artists, his work is founded in drawing, that most intimate art. And his drawing, in turn, is literally founded on the color black: Black paper is its recurrent support.

Thanks to the simple device of drawing on a black rather than a white surface, Duravcevic engineers a strange reversal: The marks he makes in graphite or pencil, which would have appeared on a white sheet as dark matter, reveal themselves instead as light, bright, reflective. This fact is not surprising—it's obvious that tone is relative— but its effects, at least in this artist's hands, often are. One feels that the image has been unearthed from the darkness. It's an illusion, of course, but not one that is intended to deceive us. No trompe l'oeil here. The drawing is always self-evidently a drawing, that is, a collection of marks on a surface. And even if whatever the drawing depicts—the head of an eagle, the flickering tongues of a flame, whatever—has been rendered with considerable realism, the motif never represents the real in the sense of nature, of the empirically observable. It is always an icon or emblem—or rather, the pictorial part of an emblem, which has been defined as "a combination of picture and text intended to draw the reader into a self-reflective examination of his or her own life." In other drawings by Duravcevic, the text itself becomes the image—but just as with his pictorial emblems, the accent is placed on the work's challenge to interpretation.

It is probably this emblematic character that accounts for the fact that in Duravcevic's work the drawn image—or the painted one—is never unique. Not only does it evoke some pre-existing model, but typically, it is repeated (often doubled). But this repetition is evidently not a case of mechanical reproduction. The image has been redrawn by hand. Though the differences are minimal, one is not quite identical to the other. But neither are we confronted with an original and a copy. Even if it were the case that one drawing were made first, the other one afterward—but it is not at all clear that this is the case; if anything, it seems more likely that the two (or more) versions of the image were made side by side, simultaneously—the first one would not be an original but always already a copy; the fact that the image seems familiar is part of its message. This is particularly clear in a group of fifty drawings of eagles' heads, some of which I recently saw in the artist's studio in Brooklyn. The eagle is, of course, the emblematic bird of the United States—a reference emphasized by the fact that there are fifty of them—but its symbolic reach is far broader: the eagle has been associated with power and conquest at least since the time of the ancient Greeks, when it was associated with Zeus. In contemporary art one thinks especially of Marcel Broodthaers and his *Museum of Modern Art, Department of Eagles*. Duravcevic's eagle looks fierce and vigilant, as sharp-eyed as legend would have it, but the marks that conjure it on the paper are as delicate as breath itself. It's almost baffling, how someone could recreate the same image with such sensitivity time after time.

And time is of the essence. Probably it is this question of time that underlies Duravcevic's art and its profound affinity with the phenomenon of repetition. Repetition is time, the inexorable ticking of the clock, in which our perceptual apparatus implants the nonexistent difference between "tick" and "tock". But does time-as-repetition reinforce the image, disintegrate it, or somehow both at once? It's a mystery, *"Il tempo è il giudice più crudele dell'arte,"* Duravcevic once told an interviewer, at the time when his work was shown in the Montenegrin pavilion in the 2015 Venice Biennale: Time is the cruelest judge of art. He's right, of course: Time sentences most art to oblivion. But it works both ways: Art is also the cruelest judge of time. Time undermines the apparent solidity of objects and monuments and reveals it to be an illusion, but the image, which persists in the absence of its referent and after the demise of its creator, breaks free of time's constraints and suggests that its inexorability, too, may be illusory. The image-world is the realm of simultaneity. I always think of something the great Italian artist Giulio Paolini once said: "Every work of art is already in itself a museum." That means that, however simple, however immediate it may seem, the work collects and preserves within itself many moments— moments in the process of its ideation and making, moments in the life of the imagination of the artist who made it, moments in the vast and almost unknowable history (artistic and otherwise) that made the artist and the work possible. In this simultaneity, time stops, or turns out to be something completely other than what we thought. "Everything feels like a déjà vu," as Duravcevic once said of the veils and fragments of the past that eternally return in his work. What once occurred, occurs again: the past recaptured? No, in this work, the past recaptures us.

Winter (tiger), 2016

Touch me not, 2016

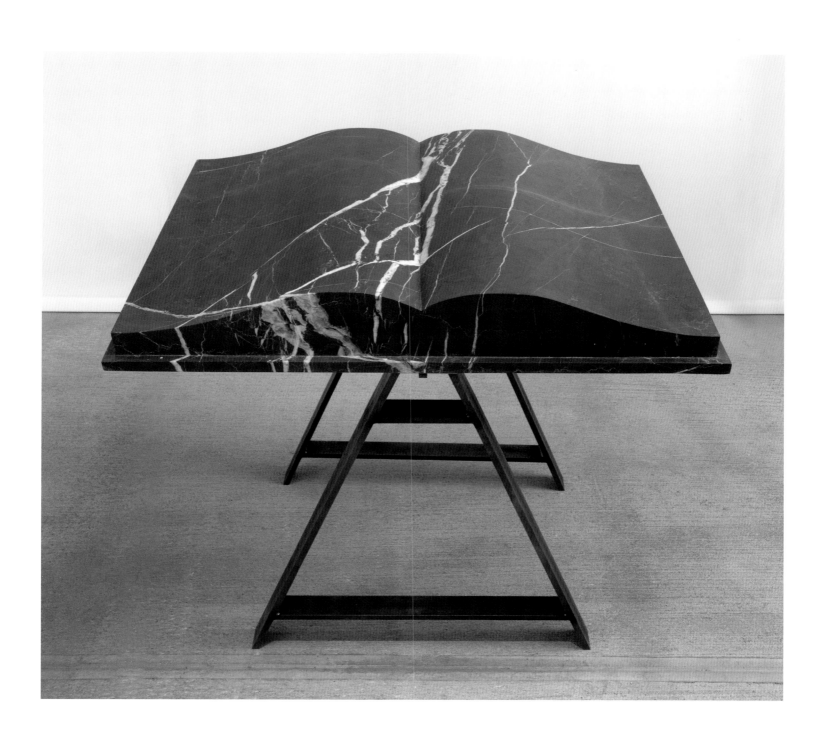

Somewhere, 2008/2012

Touch me not (hands), 2016 (diptych)

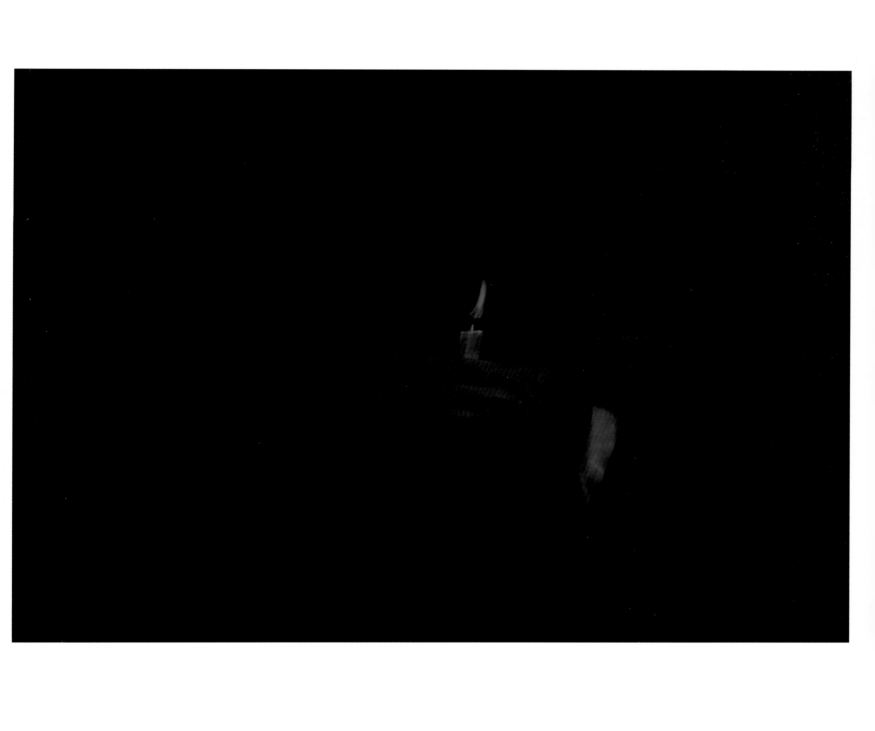

Little dancer, 2016

Untitled (Fragments), 2016

Youth, 2016

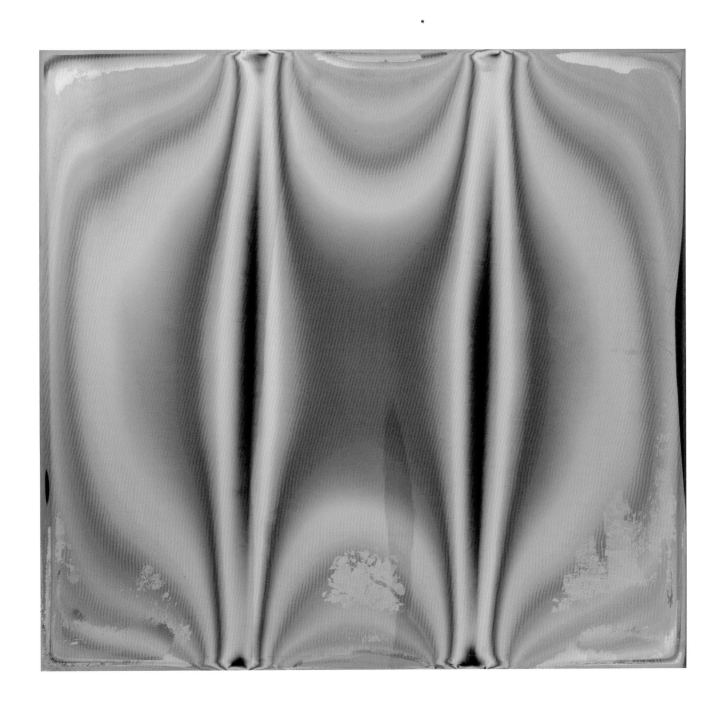

Ceiling, 2016 (diptych)

Room no. 3, 2016

Untitled/The 11, 2016

Double life, 2016 (diptych)

Youth, 2016

Untitled (fires), 2016 (diptych)

Youth, 2016

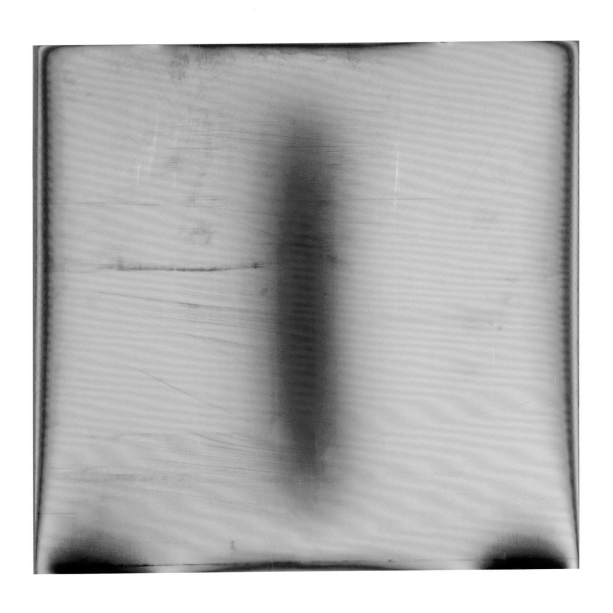

Spring (tiger), 2016

Windy Vortex

By JEREMY SIGLER

After numerous recent exchanges with Aleksandar Duravcevic—in a cab back to Brooklyn; in front of ghostly drawings in his Gowanus studio; on the telephone after being woken from a nap one afternoon; through a chain of texts and e-mails—I have come to think of his art less as a body of autonomous works than as a conversation.

In the song 'New York Telephone Conversation' off the 1972 album *Transformer*, Lou Reed describes the type of gossip associated with long nights partying and even longer mornings recovering.

> who has touched and who has dabbled
> here in the city of shows
> openings closing bad repartee
> everybody knows

But this Page-Six-ish summation of a night out on the town, is not the kind of conversation I have in mind. My evolving conversation with Duravcevic neither "rattle(s) in my head" (another lyric from Reed's song) nor indulges in scandals known only to those already "in the know". On the contrary, much of this conversation remains unknown and frankly unknowable, even as we struggle to say what we think we know and struggle to know what we think we say.

Duravcevic, in this way, may be thought of as a "method conversationist," like a method actor, training to use his emotions to unlock ours. Conversation—an art form unto itself—may thus be thought of as a practice, a skill, requiring accuracy and precision—what I would call "emotional tactics". It is what Duravcevic in one of our chats described as a life spent deep in the forest, hiding behind trees, setting one glorious trap after the next.

Duravcevic's remark speaks to the diptych of two Bengal tigers he was painting when I last visited his studio. In the panels we are oriented behind two nearly identical tigers as if peering over each one's shoulder. How unusual it is, not to be face to face with the blood-thirsty beasts; on the contrary, Duravcevic has given us the upper hand. It is the tiger, who senses the predator's gaze and breath, and it is ostensibly the viewer, who is the predator.

The mere mention of tigers in this context reminds me of Ang Lee's 2000 landmark film *Crouching Tiger Hidden Dragon*, which takes its title from an ancient Chinese idiom (or poem, originally) that contemplates a place densely populated with camouflaged, imperceivable "masters". (In this case, I suppose we would be speaking of Brooklyn, with its enormous demographic of recent art-school "Masters" also known as "M.F.A.s".) It was the poet Yu Xin who first articulated one of these tigers—one of these masterful killers—hiding in the dark behind a rock amidst the coiling dragon-like roots of giant trees.

In Lee's ballet of a kung fu film, famous for its choreographed aerial sword fights, there is one dialogue between two of the female protagonists, Jen Yu and Shu Lien, that seems to be speaking Duravcevic's language. Jen Yu yanks the sword from its sheath, and admiringly says to her competitor: "It must be exciting to be a fighter, to be totally free!" Shu Lien replies, "Fighters have rules too: friendship, trust, integrity... without rules, we wouldn't survive for long." Perhaps Duravcevic's title could conceivably be nicknamed "Crouching Artist Hidden Viewer"—a proper description of his martial art of emotion.

Indeed, setting a trap to capture another's empathy may be the goal of a noble warrior. However, just as noble is the audience's willingness to be trapped (our willful suspension of disbelief)—the pay off for our training in listening for the feeling in the story and our ability to recognize its authenticity.

I taught a class once called 'How to be a Protagonist'. In it we concentrated on subtle moments in documentary films when speakers found themselves unable to hold back tears. A famous one was in *The War Room* (D.A. Pennebaker, Chris Hegedus, 1993), when a sobbing James Carville delivers a kind of locker room speech expressing deep gratitude to his team of campaigners during their fight to get Bill Clinton elected in the 1992 primaries.

We also studied the innate pathos some performers seem to possess that can rupture before their audience. In the Gram Parsons documentary *Fallen Angel* there is a litany of testimonials to Parson's bred-in-the-bone sadness. In it, the self-proclaimed "#1 Flying Burrito Brothers Fan," Pamela Des Barres, says:

> The most memorable show I saw was at the Whiskey, and Gram was doing 'She Once Lived Here', a George Jones song. And I guess it was the bridge ("I see her face in the cool of the evening, I hear her voice with each breath loud and clear")... and tears were coming down his face singing this thing, and no one was noticing. And for me, it was my peak PEAK rock-and-roll moment. Not sitting on Jimmy Page's amp. Not dancing in the Foxy Lady video. THAT was my peak moment.[1]

Duravcevic's "coming of age" is still coming, and in many ways, coming *back* to haunt us all. As nostalgic as he can be, he also injects his past with a compelling sense of danger, that of his upbringing in Montenegro, a tribal society that conceived of every man as a free warrior, without lords, owners, or laws—except for the tribal law of blood.

Montenegro had this mystique right up to the early 90's, at the outbreak of the catastrophic Balkan War. — Duravcevic finally managed to escape to a less tribal and thus far less bloody Florence.

Within four years, Duravcevic was established in New York, where—hard as it was for any young artist to break in, due, in part, to the recession—he found himself in the highly creative ethos of multiculturalism, with artistic license and all the time in the world to "tell" his story. The detours, delays and displacements, you might say, enhanced the flavor of his slow-cooked art. "I was a late bloomer," says the artist, speaking from the perspective of a man in his mid-forties.

Duravcevic's conversation is not only a function of autobiography; it is also a function of quotation. His e-mail attachments often deliver mind-tingling aphorisms. Take for example this fragment from Mark Rothko that above and beyond all else, art must have "a clear preoccupation with death." And Euripides' reflection on how the god of wine "gently, gradually, wraps us in shadows of ivy-cool sleep." Or from Dostoyevsky, the observation that "time isn't a thing it's an idea. It'll die out in the mind." While Calvino conceives of a "poetry of the invisible, of infinite unexpected possibilities—even the poetry of nothingness." And Tarkovsky once proposed that "The present slips and vanishes like sand between the fingers, acquiring material weight only in its recollection."

Any one of these quotes, on its own, is apt to provoke thought and insight, but together they have the power to thrust a conversation—any conversation—way out into the cosmos, into a metaphysical quagmire, fueling a dialogue not between two contemporaries but between the present and past, and ultimately, between the living and the dead. Indeed, Duravcevic has an ample supply of Rothko's main required ingredient.

Consider his graphite drawings of white fire on black paper, which exhibit far more than a skillful rendering, far more than the anatomy of fire. They conflate the human source of warmth with the haunting chill of the morgue. In fact, when I first saw the drawings, it didn't even occur to me that they were depictions of fire. I didn't see flames so much as windy vortexes—ghosts. I'm reminded of Edvard Munch's *Self Portrait with Cigarette* (1895), where—caught up in the pathos of Munch's gloomy persona—one might begin to hallucinate, and see the smoke rising from the tip of his cigarette as the angel of death.

Existential and "out there," as it may be, this dialogue is also comforting and close-to-home, a casual sport played between two men wrapped in the drunken shadows of Brooklyn, volleying historic voices of invisible poetry as grains of time slip by. Quotation, in this enigmatic climate, functions as nourishment. Or as a vessel to traverse a dark sea. (Here I refer obliquely to a new sculpture by Duravcevic, a large cast sheet of black crumpled paper that, to my eye at least, symbolizes a transcontinental oceanic voyage, an odyssey.)

Compelling as such artworks are, one need not consume artworks to absorb the souls of their makers. Resolved artworks are set down in galleries or museums to bask in the glory of their own presence, proud as they are to be made. But the work's emotion may in fact stream in and flood the poetic context from other sources (and just as quickly evaporate).

The visual artist, the sculptor, is compelled to make objects and expose the world to these objects, but emotion is a free-form conversation that actually accumulates and morphs in the interstices between exposal, disposal and proposal.

The art that we see and collect is a matter of exposal; how then are we to think about proposal? A few summers ago, Duravcevic proposed tossing thousands of paper airplanes from the roof of the pavilion for the Venice Biennale. But this proposal was shot down. And he spoke to me the other day of a proposal for his upcoming show at TOTAH—a pipe organ made from a room full of empty artillery shells, before nervously changing the topic to other more tangible works in the studio that had already been green lighted. I sensed that this work was still in the dream stage, too delicate to be sacrificed to the ravenous appetite of talk.

When I asked Duravcevic about the details of this proposed artillery shell pipe organ, he said: "There will be compressed air blowing over the top on an angle like blowing into a beer bottle, producing vibrations... the air will bounce back making the shell ring. It will probably be just a single artillery shell, and the sound will ricochet for only 30 seconds." This description was accompanied by a sketch, showing not one but three shells (in his earlier proposal this had been expressed as an entire room of shells, a la Walter De Maria), and in my idealizing mind the tone was just as serial and eternal as La Monte Young's *Dream House*.

In this conversation, the disposed proposal (or the proposed disposal) begins to loop in my mind and buzz with life. I can feel myself blowing a breath of air across the smooth elliptical glass rim of an empty beer bottle. I can imagine a large hollow shell standing upright at about knee height, an empty metal container potentially filled with enough ammo to blast a car into midair, turning three human bodies into a spattered fillet of shredded flesh and bones in a pool of crimson gravy. Then I hear the pipe organ.

Proposals are off to the races. Such is the nature of the imagination. It is one more way that the artist's work comes to be realized, and that the artist's fascinations come to be contoured. Duravcevic is a maker of actual things in a studio full of materials, but his solitude is embraced by the chorus of voices in his head joined by the chorus in my head. By conversing with the artist, one may—if you listen closely—hear the entire choir.

And yet, pumped full of lyricism as this conversation may be, it may serve to lead us further from clarity and deeper into ambiguity. When I asked Duravcevic about his new series of *Youth* pieces—fishing, as I was, for exact specification in order to explain the work in this essay—he guided me to indeed a murky place. What appeared as a suicide-proof, prison mirror in stainless steel (with an inexplicable rainbow effect like gasoline on pavement), was described as: "somewhat a mirror well to look back through a cloud of color... like dreaming with your eyes open." Duravcevic could have just said: "it is only a dream," like the American song writer Stephen Foster wrote in his famous parlor song from 1862 'Beautiful Dreamer'. The final stanza goes like this:

> Beautiful dreamer, beam on my heart,
> Even as the morn on the streamlet and sea;
> Then will all clouds of sorrow depart,
> Beautiful dreamer, awake unto me!

Two summers ago in 2015, Aleksandar Duravcevic had an exhibition in the 56th Biennale di Venezia in the Montenegro Pavilion. It was a big occasion. As I mentioned before, his initial paper airplane proposal was not accepted, but he persevered with an installation of numerous sculptures, drawings, paintings, and video works, all commanding the pavilion and demanding energy from the viewer. The show provided a public with numerous engaging artworks, though I was not among the jet-lagged cultural gypsies who witnessed it.

But I have nevertheless post-facto found an interest in projecting myself into/onto one of the works in the show, itself a projection, entitled *Waiting* (2015). The video, which was viewed hovering on the exterior wall of the pavilion, high up and easy to miss, showed an old lady in black doing nothing more than leaning on the windowsill passing the time away (a "Fresh Widow," to recall Rose Sélavy's 1920 pun on "French Window").

What was this fresh widow doing, other than smoking a cigarette (like Munch's self portrait)? She was neither there to watch, nor to be watched. She was neither there to see, nor to be seen. She was a default artwork. She was merely coexisting with her companion: the window frame. This window was, in a sense, all that she had. It was like an extension of her anatomy. Like passing out in bed with your shoes on.

Indeed the widow is waiting at the window, but unlike the two chatterboxes in Beckett's comedy, Vladimir and Estragon, she is silent. If she is an example of minimalist theater, then I'd propose that Duravcevic has cleverly assigned her a non-speaking part in a zero-act play with no lines.

But I'm more reminded of the existential comedy, by Jerzy Kosinsky, *Being There*. Not of the characters and lines, per se, but of the book's (and film's) title. The old woman is where? She is not down with the art-work and art-world, but up where the works and viewers are not. The title allows us to gaze down "there" upon the world and to fixate on the ordinary machinations of life.

The woman is thus an allegory for death, she is one of the three fates, similar to the two fates that appear in Joseph Conrad's *Heart of Darkness*. Marlow encounters these two women-in-black before heading out on his mission to retrieve the rogue:

> She seemed to know all about them and about me too. An eerie feeling came over me. She seemed uncanny and fateful. Often far away there I thought of these two, guarding the door of Darkness, knitting black wool as for a warm pall, one introducing, introducing continuously to the unknown, the other scrutinizing the cheery and foolish faces with unconcerned old eyes.[2]

Duravcevic's widow, just like Conrad's (not to mention his two flames and three angelic artillery shells) feels like a cryptic, perhaps even unconscious reference to the Moirae—the three fates of ancient Greek lore who spin our life threads and, unfortunately for us, cut them at the moment of their choosing.

At TOTAH is another work obsessed with Rothkoesque mortality. It is a brooding new sculpture called *Touch me not* (2016). It is a representation in stone of a very big and very heavy book. But it is not a book—there are no pages, nor a single word, hieroglyph, inscription, illustration, caption, contents or colophon. There is no front cover, back cover, nor spine. It is in the shape of a big open book, but it comes off more like an ancient tablet, albeit a tablet with nothing on it.

Nevertheless we read it. We read its saga, its geology. We read its white lines, the veins that splinter though its mass like abstract expressionist lightning bolts.

Touch me not (big book) is impersonal (closed), yet deeply emotional (an open book if there ever was one). Perhaps it is an externalization, a palpable marker of a fleeting emotion.

Consider Moses' bestseller *The Ten Commandments* (see Rembrandt's 1659 painting *Moses Breaking the Tablets of the Law*). This read, essential to the reading list of any moralist, is still being digested by some, and understood by others. In *Crime and Punishment*, Raskolnikov grapples with "the basic 10" when he decides to test out his "extraordinary man" theory on the old pawn broker (just the other day, Dylann Roof defeated the big black book (he is apparently neither insane nor stricken with guilt). Since the Enlightenment, writers have asked: is "thou shalt not kill" inside us at birth? Or does morality seep in over time, like mineral deposits in stone?

Duravcevic's gravestone book—like the woman in black at her window, like the flaming ghost, like the crumpled sea, like the moaning shells—seems to mark and remark on emotions that cannot be held back. At least that's what I gather from the conversation. But how do you see it?

[1] see Gram Parsons: Fallen Angel, directed by Gandulf Hennig (2004).

[2] Joseph Conrad, Heart of Darkness, Fifth Critical Edition, W. W. Norton & Company, Aug. 29, 2016.

Eastern wind, 2012, Installation

List of Plates

Winter (tiger)
2016
Oil paint on linen mounted on board
72 x 48 inches (183 x 122 cm)

Touch me not (hands)
2016 (diptych)
Graphite on paper
20 x 28, 28 x 40 inches (51 x 71, 71 x 101 cm)

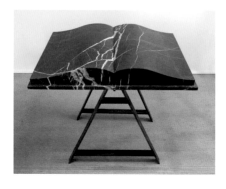

Touch me not
2016
Graphite stone, pedestal
20 x 30 inches (51 x 76 cm)

Little dancer (skull)
2016
Carrara stone
18 x 18 inches (45 x 45 cm)

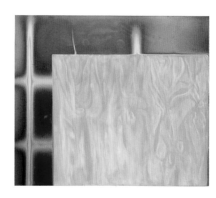

Somewhere
2008/2012
Chemically treated stainless steel, oil paint
43 x 48 inches (109 x 122 cm)

Untitled (fragments)
2016
Graphite on paper
28 x 40 inches (71 x 101 cm)

Youth
2016
Chemically treated stainless steel
24 x 24 inches (61 x 61 cm)

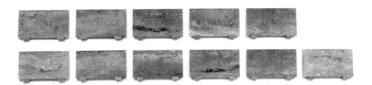

Untitled/The 11
2016
Engraved travertine
13 x 22 1/2 inches (33 x 57 cm)

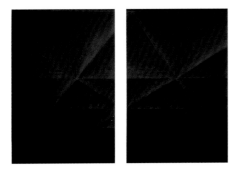

Ceiling
2016 (diptych)
Graphite on paper
95 x 62 inches (241 cm x 157 cm)

Double life
2016 (diptych)
Oil paint on icon board
11 x 15 inches (28 x 38 cm)

Room no. 3
2016
Cast resin, graphite
111 x 51 inches (282 x 129 cm)

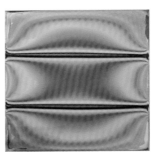

Youth
2016
Chemically treated stainless steel
24 x 24 inches (61 x 61 cm)

List of Plates

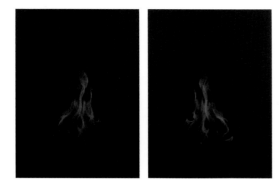

Untitled (fires)
2016 (diptych)
Graphite on paper
28 x 40 inches (71 x 101 cm)

Spring (tiger)
2016
Oil paint on linen mounted on board
72 x 48 inches (183 x 122 cm)

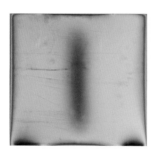

Youth
2016
Chemically treated stainless steel
15 x 15 inches (38 x 38 cm)

Eastern wind
2012
Installation, variable sizes
Artillery shells (brass), air control/compressor

ALEKSANDAR DURAVCEVIC

born 1970 in Montenegro
Lives and works in Brooklyn, New York
1990-1992 University of Montenegro "Veljko Vlahović", Faculty of Arts, Cetinje
1992-1993 Accademia di Bella Arte, Florence, Italy
1993-1995 Scuola di Arte Grafica "IL Bisonte", Florence, Italy
1999 MFA Pratt Institute, New York

2017

Steppenwolf, Totah, New York
Three Positions. Six Directions. | Chapter II: Door to the Future, Window to the Past, König
Galerie, Berlin, Germany
Group Show, Totah, New York

2015

Ti Ricordi Sjecas Li Se You Remember, 56th International Art Exibition - La Biennale di
Venezia 2015, National Participation, Palazzo MaliPiero, Pavilion of Montenegro, Italy
Aleksandar Duravcevic Selected Works, R/E Projects, Madrid, Spain
Without Words, curated by Osvaldo Romberg, Pennsylvania Academy of Fine Arts,
Philadelphia, Pennsylvania
Theorem, curated by Octavio Zaya, Mana Contemporary, Jersey City, New Jersey

2014

New Work, Sala Gaspar, Barcelona, Spain
Aleksandar Duravcevic, Fundación Antonio Perez, Cuenca, Spain
Aleksandar Duravcevic Selected Works, Petrovic Palace, Center of Contemporary Art,
Montenegro, Dvorac Petrovica, Centar Savremene Umijetnosti, Montenegro
Treed, Altana, KulturStiftung Foundation, Hamburg, Germany
Politics of Drawings, curated by Philip Glahn, Sarah Lawrence College, New York, New York
Mirror Mirror, Galerie Stefan Röpke, Cologne, Germany
Expanded Drawing 014, Casal Solleric, Palma de Mallorca, Spain

2013

Room No 1, Armory show, Solo project, New York, USA

2012

Tell Me Yours I Will Tell You Mine, Galería Arnés y Röpke, Madrid, Spain
Tell Me Yours I Will Tell You Mine, Galerie Stefan Röpke, Cologne, Germany
Baccanalia, Landrum Presents, London, England
Expanded Drawing 012, Casal Solleric, Palma de Mallorca, Spain
Site/109 with Galerie Stefan Röpke, New York, New York, USA
Galerie Stefan Röpke, Cologne, Germany

2011

Brooklyn Ball, Brooklyn Museum of Art, New York, New York, USA
Skin, Galerie Stefan Röpke, Cologne, Germany

2010

The Light of the Crystal, Museum für Gestaltung, Zurich, Switzerland
Arario Gallery, New York, New York
Pulse Special Projects, New York, New York

2009

Aleksandar Duravcevic, MUSEO AB 23, Contenitore per il contemporaneo, Vincenza, Italy
Restless, Galerie Stefan Röpke, Cologne, Germany
Anna Kustera Gallery, New York, New York
Dream World and the Castles in the Sky, Castle Gaasbeek, Brussels, Belgium
Galería Arnés y Röpke, Madrid, Spain
Publications of VFG, Brooklyn Museum of Art, New York, New York

2008

Home Again, Kuslevova Kuca, Museum of City of Podgorica, Montenegro

2007

New Work, Yvon Lambert Project Space, New York, New York
Houghton Library, Harvard University, Boston

2005

International Print Center, curated by Kiki Smith, New York, New York
Rubbell-Schafler Galleries, Pratt Institute, Brooklyn, New York, New York

2004

New Acquisitions, Metropolitan Museum of Art, New York, New York
International Print Center, New York, New York

2003

Uffizi Gallery, Florence, Italy
International Print Center, New York, New York

2002

Drawings and Prints, 5+5 Gallery, Brooklyn, New York

2001

Drawings and Prints, Mark Woolley Gallery, Portland

2000

Drawings and Prints, Julie Cencebaugh Contemporary, New York, New York

Made in Brooklyn Books, Drawings and Prints, Brooklyn Museum of Art, New York, New York
New Visions, Lustberg, Bridgwater and Blumenfeld, New York, New York
Greater New York, P.S.1 MOMA, Queens, New York
Museo Marino Marini, Florence, Italy

1999
Drawings and Prints, Mark Woolley Gallery, Portland
Prints and Drawings, Lustberg & Blumenfeld, New York, New York
Seeing Is Believing Age of Science, New York Public Library, New York, New York
Galeria Centro Colombo Americano, Medelin, Columbia

1997
Nicolet College, Rheinlander, Wisconsin
Parchman Stremmel Galleries, San Antonio, Texas
Staten Island Institute of Arts and Sciences, New York

1996
Museo de Arte de la Universidad Nacionale de Columbia, Bogota, Colombia
Galleria II Bisonte, Florence, Italy

SELECTED COLLECTIONS
Metropolitan Museum of Art, New York
Museum of Fine Arts, Boston
Lirik Kabinett, Munich
Munson Williams Proctor Institute, Utica, New York
The New York Public Library, New York
The Brooklyn Museum, New York
Columbia University, New York
San Francisco Public Library, San Francisco
University of Iowa, Iowa City
Springfield Museum, Missouri
Smith College, Northampton
Harvard University, Cambridge

SELECTED AWARDS
2005   New York Foundation for the Arts
1999   Pratt Institute, Excellence Award for Outstanding Merit in Graduate Fine Arts
1998   Elizabeth Greenshields Foundation, Artistic Achievement
1997   Staten Island Institute of Arts and Sciences, Award of Merit

Barry Schwabsky is an American art critic, art historian and poet. Schwabsky writes regularly on art for the Nation and co-edits international reviews for Artforum, while contributing essays to many publications, including Flash Art, London Review of Books, New Left Review and Art in America. He has taught at School of Visual Arts, Pratt Institute, New York University, Yale University, and Goldsmiths College, among others. Schwabsky is the author of *The Perpetual Guest: Art in the Unfinished Present* (2016), *Words for Art: Criticism, History, Theory, Practice* (2013), *The Widening Circle: Consequences of Modernism in Contemporary Art* (Cambridge University Press, 1997) and has contributed to *Abstract Painting: Concepts and Techniques* and *Vitamin P: New Perspectives in Painting* (Phaidon Press), in addition to monographs on artists such as Mel Bochner, Alighiero Boetti, Karin Davie, Alex Katz, R.B. Kitaj, Chloe Piene, Henri Matisse, Dana Schutz, Jessica Stockholder, Antonio Tapies, and Gillian Wearing.

Jeremy Sigler is a poet, critic and editor living in New York. Sigler holds an M.F.A in sculpture from University of California, Los Angeles and a BFA from the University of Pennsylvania. He has published six collections of poetry, *To and To* (1998), *Mallet Eyes* (2000), *Led Almost by my Tie* (2007), *Math* (2008), *Crackpot Poet* (2010), and the much acclaimed *My Vibe* (Spoonbill Books, 2017). Sigler has served as Lecturer in Sculpture at Yale University School of Arts, and was Associate Editor for the Swiss art journal *Parkett*. In 2006 Sigler was awarded a Lannan Foundation Poetry residency in Marfa. He recently co-edited *Carl Andre: Sculpture as Place, 1958–2010*, a full-career retrospective monograph on the poet-sculptor, co-published in 2014 by Dia Art Foundation and Yale University Press. Sigler's next book, *Carl Andre: Love Poet in Marxist Overalls* is due out later this year with Sternberg Press.